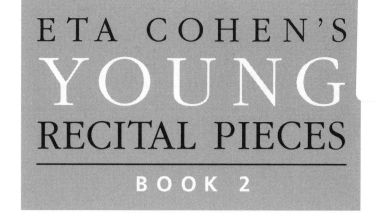

ETA COHEN'S
YOUNG
RECITAL PIECES
BOOK 2

Enjoyable repertoire for young violinists

Novello Publishing Limited
8-9 Frith Street, London W1V 5TZ

Exclusive distributors:
Music Sales Limited
Newmarket Road, Bury St Edmunds,
Suffolk IP33 3YB.
All rights reserved.

Order No. NOV916181
ISBN 0-85360-560-2
© Copyright 1996 Novello & Company Limited.
8/9 Frith Street, London W1V 5TZ.

Music set by Stave Origination.
Cover design by Xheight Limited.
Printed in the United Kingdom by
Caligraving Limited, Thetford, Norfolk.

CONTENTS

1999
Class A 3

To my daughter Anna

OUT OF CAPRICORN SUITE

1 Tin Soldiers

In the style of a march. Use *martelé* bowing for the staccato notes
and whole bows for the minims.
From bar 44 play with firm, short detached bows.

Philip Wilby

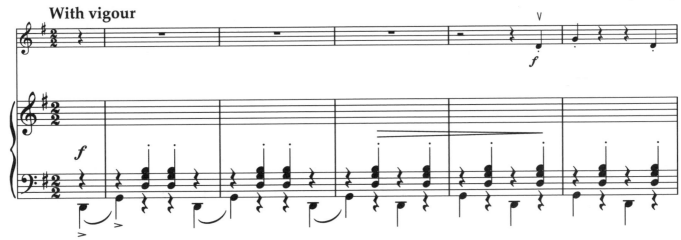

4

2 Consolation

Use whole bows for every bar and keep the piece very smooth.
Try to get a beautiful sound.

Philip Wilby

5

6

3 The Whistler's Waltz

Keep the bowing short and play at the middle of the bow.
Imagine you are accompanying a dance.
Remember to lift the bow where there are rests.

Philip Wilby

4 Rooster Rag

Martelé bowing for the staccato notes.

Philip Wilby

12

AUTUMN I

The third position is optional: the whole piece could be played in
first position if you prefer. Play brightly with very firm bows.

A. Vivaldi
From The Four Seasons

I DREAMT I DWELT IN MARBLE HALLS

Use whole bows for most bars — keep it smooth and dream-like.

M.W. Balfe
From The Bohemian Girl
Arr. Hywel Davies

SERENADE

This piece should be smooth and song-like. Play very expressively.
The third position passages can be played in first position if preferred.

F. Schubert
Arr. Hywel Davies

COMIN' THRO' THE RYE

Take great care with the timing of the dotted rhythms.

Traditional
Arr. Hywel Davies

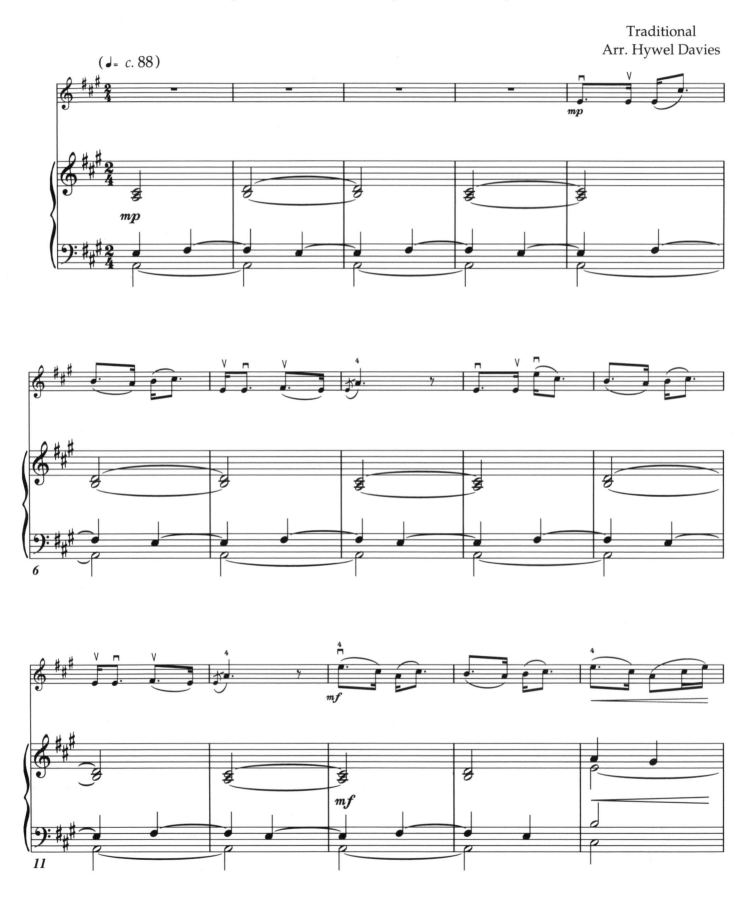

21

HUNTING CHORUS

Joyfully and with great vigour. Use short bows.

C.M. von Weber
From Der Freischütz
Arr. Hywel Davies

THE MARQUIS OF HUNTLY'S HIGHLAND FLING

Play with plenty of energy!

Traditional
Arr. Hywel Davies

MY FAITHFUL HEART, REJOICE

Try to imagine you are singing when you play this.

J.S. Bach
Arr. Hywel Davies